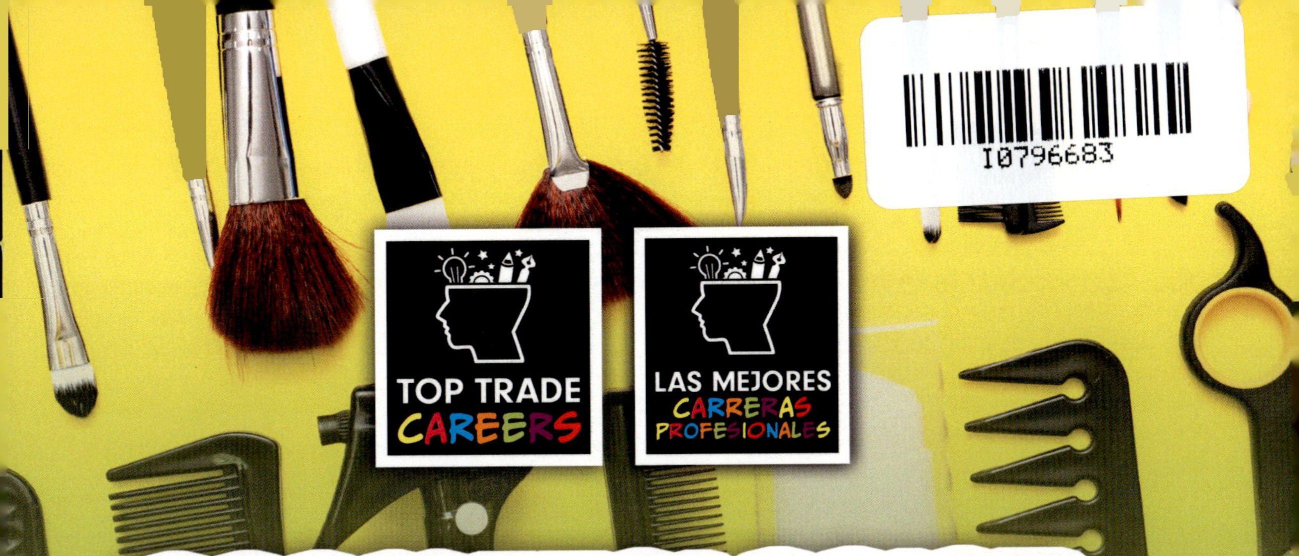

TOP TRADE CAREERS

LAS MEJORES CARRERAS PROFESIONALES

COSMETOLOGIST
COSMETÓLOGO

A Crabtree Branches Book
Un libro de Las Ramas de Crabtree

Written by / Escrito por Kelli Hicks
Translated by / Traducción de Santiago Ochoa

School-to-Home Support for Caregivers and Teachers

This high-interest book is designed to motivate striving students with engaging topics while building fluency, vocabulary, and an interest in reading. Here are a few questions and activities to help the reader build upon his or her comprehension skills.

Before Reading:

- *What do I think this book is about?*
- *What do I know about this topic?*
- *What do I want to learn about this topic?*
- *Why am I reading this book?*

During Reading:

- *I wonder why...*
- *I'm curious to know...*
- *How is this like something I already know?*
- *What have I learned so far?*

After Reading:

- *What was the author trying to teach me?*
- *What are some details?*
- *How did the photographs and captions help me understand more?*
- *Read the book again and look for the vocabulary words.*
- *What questions do I still have?*

Extension Activities:

- *What was your favorite part of the book? Write a paragraph on it.*
- *Draw a picture of your favorite thing you learned from the book.*

Apoyo escolar para cuidadores y maestros

Este libro de alto interés está diseñado para motivar a los estudiantes dedicados con temas atractivos, mientras desarrollan la fluidez, el vocabulario y el interés por la lectura. A continuación se presentan algunas preguntas y actividades para ayudar al lector a desarrollar sus habilidades de comprensión.

Antes de leer:

- *¿De qué pienso que trata este libro?*
- *¿Qué sé sobre este tema?*
- *¿Qué quiero aprender sobre este tema?*
- *¿Por qué estoy leyendo este libro?*

Durante la lectura:

- *Me pregunto por qué...*
- *Tengo curiosidad de saber...*
- *¿En qué se parece esto a algo que ya conozco?*
- *¿Qué he aprendido hasta ahora?*

Después de leer:

- *¿Qué intentaba enseñarme el autor?*
- *¿Cuáles son algunos detalles?*
- *¿Cómo me ayudaron las fotografías y los pies de foto a entender más?*
- *Vuelve a leer el libro y busca las palabras del vocabulario.*
- *¿Qué preguntas tengo aún?*

Actividades de extensión:

- *¿Cuál fue tu parte favorita del libro? Escribe un párrafo sobre ella.*
- *Haz un dibujo de lo que más te gustó del libro.*

TABLE OF CONTENTS

ÍNDICE

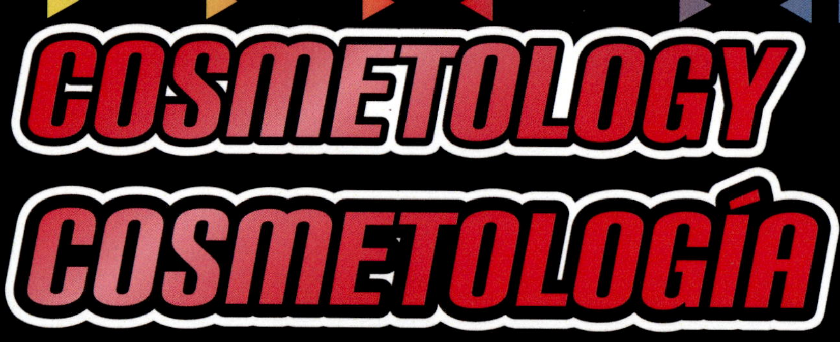

COSMETOLOGY COSMETOLOGÍA

Many people work in a community. A teacher helps students learn and a mechanic fixes cars. Other community members are important, too.

Muchas personas trabajan en una comunidad. Un profesor ayuda a los alumnos a aprender y un mecánico arregla autos. Otros miembros de la comunidad también son importantes.

Have you heard of a cosmetologist? Cosmetologists are **professionals** who help people look and feel their best.

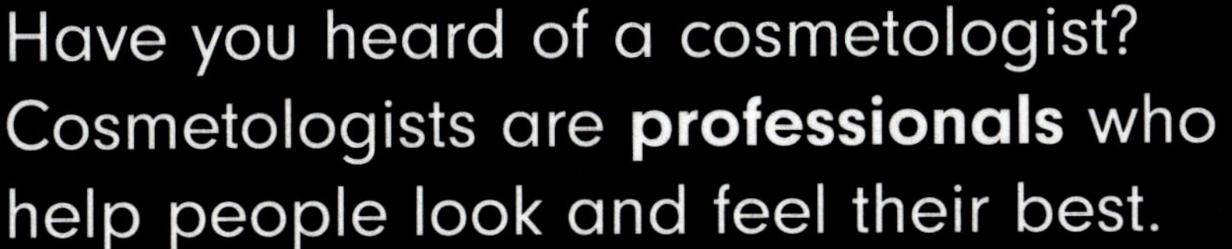

¿Has oído hablar de los cosmetólogos? Los cosmetólogos son **profesionales** que ayudan a las personas a verse y sentirse mejor.

Do you need a new hairstyle or have issues with your skin? Did you get a part in a play and need to look like someone else? Do you want to find out the latest **trends**? A cosmetologist is just what you need.

¿Necesitas un nuevo peinado o tienes problemas con tu piel? ¿Te dieron un papel en una obra de teatro y necesitas parecerte a otra persona? ¿Quieres conocer las últimas **tendencias**? Un cosmetólogo es justo lo que necesitas.

There are many jobs in the field of cosmetology, and each one helps you in a different way.

Hay muchos trabajos en el campo de la cosmetología y cada uno de ellos te ayuda de una manera diferente.

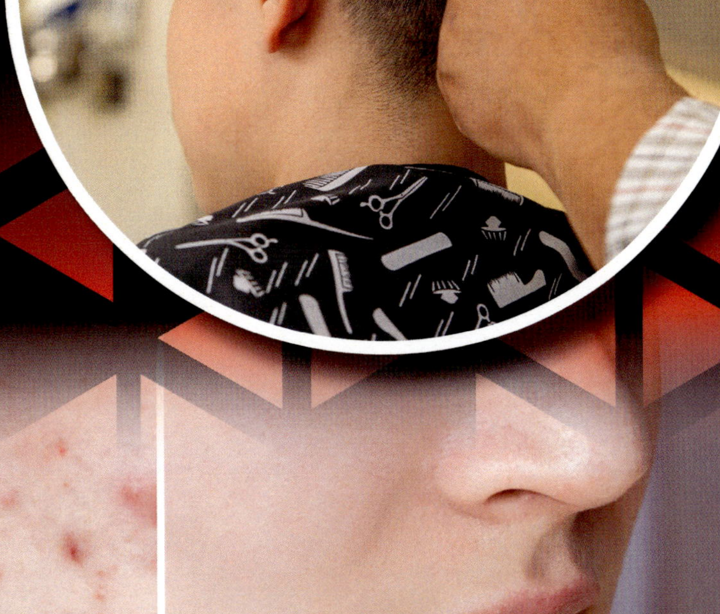

Estheticians are skin-care professionals who have studied cosmetology. They usually work in spas or clinics.

Los esteticistas son profesionales del cuidado de la piel que han estudiado cosmetología. Suelen trabajar en spas o clínicas.

CARING FOR HAIR

EL CUIDADO DEL CABELLO

A hairdresser cuts and styles hair. This **specialist** can safely change hair color, too. Hairdressers use scissors, clippers, and special products to take care of hair.

Un peluquero corta y peina el cabello. Este **especialista** también puede cambiar el color del cabello de forma segura. Los peluqueros utilizan tijeras, maquinillas y productos especiales para cuidar el cabello.

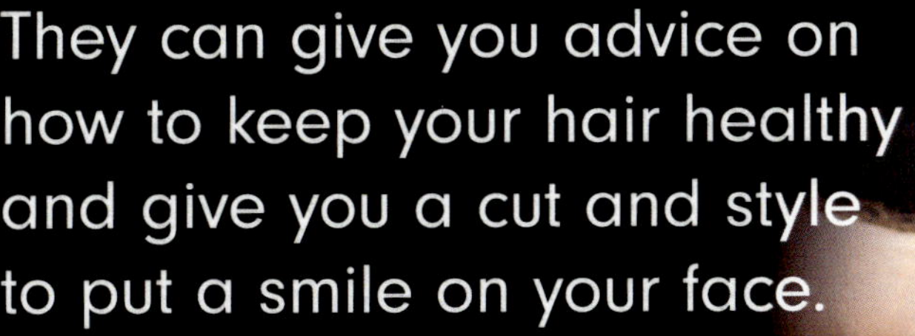

They can give you advice on how to keep your hair healthy and give you a cut and style to put a smile on your face.

Pueden aconsejarte sobre cómo mantener tu pelo sano y hacerte un corte y un peinado que te haga sonreír.

Kristin Ess is a social media influencer who grew up in a family of ten children. She always knew she wanted to work in the beauty industry. She got a job in a Beverly Hills, California, salon and styled the hair of celebrities. She has a huge following online and created her own line of hair products. She believes honesty and hard work will help you be a success.

Kristin Ess es una *influencer* de las redes sociales que creció en una familia de diez hijos. Siempre supo que quería trabajar en la industria de la belleza. Consiguió un trabajo en un salón de belleza de Beverly Hills, California, y peinó a celebridades. Tiene muchos seguidores en Internet y ha creado su propia línea de productos capilares. Cree que la honestidad y el trabajo duro te ayudan a tener éxito.

A barber has a similar job to a hairdresser, but focuses on services for boys and men. Barbers have skill to create styles that look great.

Un barbero tiene un trabajo similar al de un peluquero, pero se centra en servicios para niños y hombres. Los barberos tienen la habilidad de crear estilos que se vean bien.

Barbers also trim beards and mustaches. In some communities, the barbershop is a place to **socialize** and catch up on the news.

Los barberos también recortan barbas y bigotes. En algunas comunidades, la barbería es un lugar para **socializar** y ponerse al día.

Over 500 years ago, barbers did more than cut hair. They pulled teeth, treated wounds, and set broken bones. Called barber-surgeons, they used their skill with sharp tools to perform medical procedures.

Hace más de 500 años, los barberos hacían algo más que cortar el pelo. Sacaban dientes, curaban heridas y componían huesos rotos. Llamados barberos-cirujanos, utilizaban su habilidad con herramientas afiladas para realizar procedimientos médicos.

PEDICURE, PLEASE
PEDICURA, POR FAVOR

A nail **technician** is a skilled worker trained to trim, paint, and restore the health of your hands and toes. A manicure takes care of your fingernails and hands, while a pedicure focuses on your feet.

Un **técnico** de uñas es un trabajador capacitado para recortar, pintar y restaurar la salud de las manos y los dedos de los pies. La manicura se ocupa de las uñas y las manos, mientras que la pedicura se centra en los pies.

The nail technician is unable to treat medical conditions, but can give you advice on dealing with minor nail problems.

El técnico de uñas no puede tratar afecciones médicas, pero puede aconsejarte sobre cómo tratar problemas menores en las uñas.

MIGHTY MAKE-UP MAQUILLAJE DE LUJO

Make-up artists focus on skin care and the **application** of make-up. Some instruct people about the best products to keep their skin clean and healthy.

Los maquilladores se centran en el cuidado de la piel y la **aplicación** del maquillaje. Algunos instruyen a las personas sobre los mejores productos para mantener su piel limpia y sana.

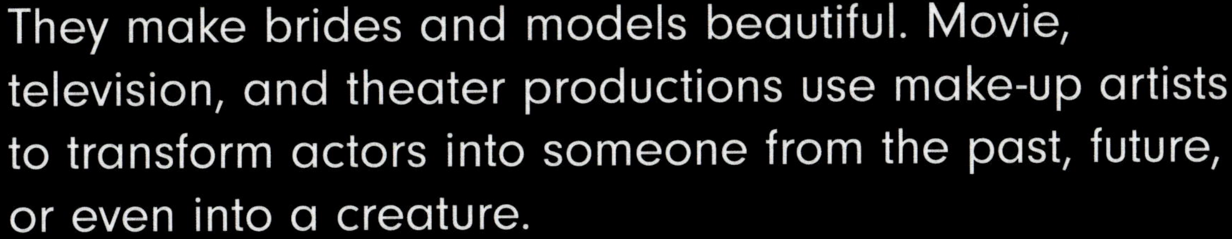

They make brides and models beautiful. Movie, television, and theater productions use make-up artists to transform actors into someone from the past, future, or even into a creature.

Hacen que las novias y las modelos sean bellas. Las producciones de cine, televisión y teatro utilizan a los maquilladores para transformar a los actores en alguien del pasado, del futuro o incluso en una criatura.

INFLUENCE AND STYLE
INFLUENCIA Y ESTILO

Many cosmetologists use social media to educate people on health and beauty trends. It is a great way to gain customers and to influence trends in hair, nail, and skin care.

Muchos cosmetólogos utilizan las redes sociales para informar a la gente sobre las tendencias de salud y belleza. Es una gran manera de ganar clientes y de influir en las tendencias del cuidado del cabello, las uñas y la piel.

Some cosmetologists become personal stylists. They design hair and make-up for models on a photo shoot, prepare a performer for the stage, or get celebrities camera-ready for special events.

Algunos cosmetólogos se convierten en estilistas personales. Diseñan el peinado y el maquillaje para modelos en una sesión de fotos, preparan a un artista para el escenario o a las celebridades para las cámaras en eventos especiales.

Born into a military family, Ted Gibson spent many years traveling the world. He learned about the beauty of different cultures, which led him to cosmetology. He has been a hairdresser, celebrity stylist, salon owner, and social media influencer.

Nacido en una familia de militares, Ted Gibson pasó muchos años viajando por el mundo. Aprendió sobre la belleza de diferentes culturas, lo que lo llevó a la cosmetología. Ha sido peluquero, estilista de famosos, propietario de salones de belleza e *influencer* en las redes sociales.

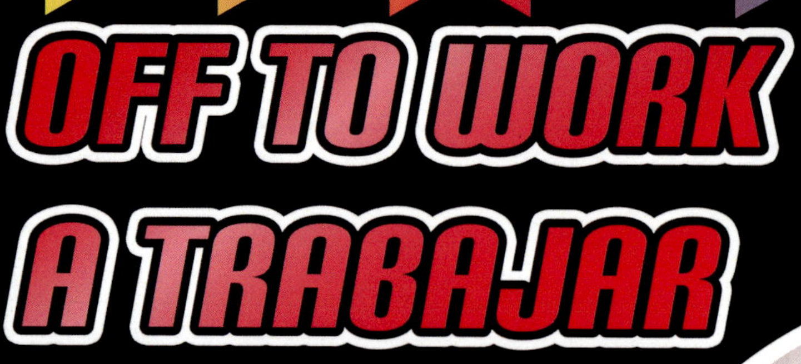

OFF TO WORK
A TRABAJAR

A cosmetologist usually works in a salon, shop, or spa. Many new cosmetologists choose to work for someone else. It is a great way to gain experience and to learn about the profession.

Un cosmetólogo suele trabajar en un salón de belleza, tienda o spa. Muchos nuevos cosmetólogos optan por trabajar para alguien. Es una buena manera de adquirir experiencia y aprender más sobre la profesión.

Some cosmetologists run their own small business or work **freelance**, sometimes in a home studio. Some travel to different locations, such as a movie set, an event center, or around the world to share their craft.

Algunos cosmetólogos dirigen su propia pequeña empresa o trabajan como **independientes**, a veces en un estudio casero. Algunos viajan a diferentes lugares, como el plató de una película, un centro de eventos o por todo el mundo para compartir su oficio.

WHERE DO I START?
¿POR DÓNDE COMIENZO?

To get started, you need to be at least 16 years old and have a high school diploma. It is important to attend a specialized school, which may only take 9–15 months to complete.

Para empezar, debes tener al menos 16 años y un título de secundaria. Es importante asistir a una escuela especializada, que puede tardar entre 9 y 15 meses en completarse.

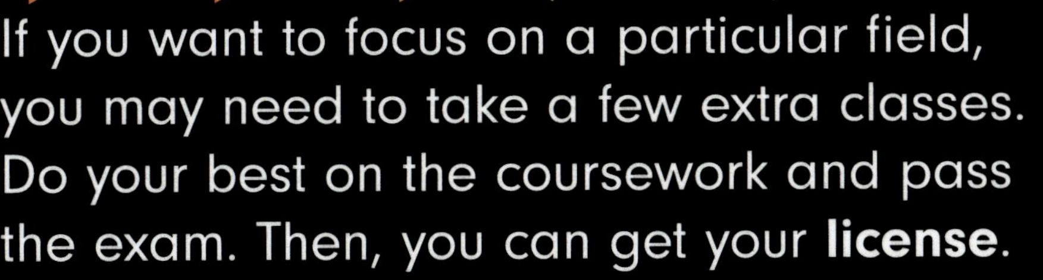

If you want to focus on a particular field, you may need to take a few extra classes. Do your best on the coursework and pass the exam. Then, you can get your **license**.

Si quieres centrarte en un campo concreto, puede que tengas que tomar algunas clases extra. Esfuérzate al máximo en los cursos y aprueba el examen. Después, podrás obtener tu **licencia**.

SPECIAL SKILLS

HABILIDADES ESPECIALES

Could you be a cosmetologist? You need to know current trends and have good grooming habits. It helps to be friendly and a good listener. Customers make appointments, so you also need to manage your time well.

¿Puedes ser cosmetólogo? Tienes que conocer las tendencias actuales y tener buenos hábitos de aseo. Ser amable y un buen oyente son dos cosas útiles. Los clientes piden citas, así que también hay que gestionar bien el tiempo.

It is important to be creative and artistic, thinking of new ideas for colors and designs. A cosmetologist always follows health and safety laws and guidelines.

Es importante ser creativo y artístico, así como pensar en nuevas ideas para los colores y los diseños. Un cosmetólogo sigue siempre las leyes y directrices de salud y seguridad.

This job can be challenging. It takes dedication and money to get a license. Cosmetologists generally stand a lot, which can be tough on your back and feet.

Este trabajo puede ser un reto. Se necesita dedicación y dinero para obtener una licencia. Los cosmetólogos suelen estar mucho tiempo de pie, lo que puede ser duro para la espalda y los pies.

Some clients can be **demanding** or difficult, so you need to have a positive attitude and be patient. Customers want to feel comfortable. It takes caring and hard work to be a success.

Algunos clientes pueden ser **exigentes** o difíciles, por lo que hay que tener una actitud positiva y ser paciente. Los clientes quieren sentirse cómodos. Se necesita ser considerado y trabajar duro para tener éxito.

HOW MUCH DO I MAKE?
¿CUÁNTO GANARÍA?

Cosmetology can be a rewarding career. Not only can you help people, but you can earn a good living as well.

Your salary may be affected by where you live, your level of experience, and whether you work for someone else or for yourself.

La cosmetología puede ser una carrera gratificante. No solo puedes ayudar a la gente, sino que también puedes tener una buena vida.

Tu salario puede verse afectado por el lugar donde vives, tu nivel de experiencia y si trabajas por cuenta propia o para alguien más.

Specialty	Salary Range Per Year
Hairdresser	$18,000 - $39,000
Barber	$20,000 - $40,000
Make-up Artist	$16,000 - $28,000
Social Media Influencer	$14,000 - $74,500
Personal Stylist	$71,000 - $91,000
Nail Technician	$16,000 - $28,000

Especialidad	Rango salarial por año en dólares
Peluquero	$18 000 - $39 000
Barbero	$20 000 - $40 000
Maquillador	$16 000 - $28 000
Influencer de redes sociales	$14 000 - $74 500
Estilista personal	$71 000 - $91 000
Técnico de uñas	$16 000 - $28 000

Cosmetologists can have a great impact on the people of a community. Their work helps people to be confident and feel good about themselves. When people feel confident, they can do almost anything!

Los cosmetólogos pueden tener un gran impacto en las personas de una comunidad. Su trabajo ayuda a las personas a tener confianza y a sentirse bien consigo mismas. Cuando las personas se sienten seguras de sí, ¡pueden hacer casi cualquier cosa!

GLOSSARY

application (ap-luh-KAY-shuhn): a way of using something

demanding (di-MAN-ding): requiring a lot of time, attention, or effort

freelance (FREE-lanss): getting paid for individual jobs

license (LYE-suhnss): a document giving you permission to do something

professionals (pruh-FESH-uh-nuhlz): members of an occupation that have specialized skills or training

social media (SOH-shuhl MEE-dee-uh): a form of electronic communication to share ideas, thoughts, and information

socialize (SOH-shuhl-eyez): getting together with people in a friendly way

specialist (SPESH-uh-list): an expert at one particular job or area

technician (tek-NISH-uhn): someone who works with specialized equipment

trends (trendz): the latest fashions

GLOSARIO

aplicación: Forma de utilizar algo.

especialista: Experto en un trabajo o área en particular.

exigentes: Que requieren mucho tiempo, atención o esfuerzo.

independientes: Que cobran por trabajos individuales.

licencia: Documento que da permiso para hacer algo.

profesionales: Miembros de una ocupación que tienen habilidades o formación especializada.

redes sociales: Forma de comunicación electrónica para compartir ideas, pensamientos e información.

socializar: Reunirse con personas de forma amistosa.

técnico: Alguien que trabaja con equipos especializados.

tendencias: La última moda.

INDEX

ÍNDICE ANALÍTICO

WEBSITES TO VISIT
SITIOS WEB PARA VISITAR

www.thebalancecareers.com/cosmetology-careers-524866

www.beautyschoolsdirectory.com/programs/cosmetology-school

https://elitebeautysociety.com/cosmetology-school

ABOUT THE AUTHOR

Kelli Hicks is a teacher and writer who lives in Florida with her husband and two children. She likes the relaxation of visiting her hairdresser and appreciates the patience her hairdresser takes in dealing with her wild and crazy hair.

SOBRE LA AUTORA

Kelli Hicks es una profesora y escritora que vive con su familia en Florida. Le gusta la relajación de visitar a su peluquero y aprecia la paciencia que este tiene al tratar con su pelo incontrolable y rebelde.

Crabtree Publishing

crabtreebooks.com 800-387-7650

Written by/Escrito por: Kelli Hicks
Designer/Diseñadora: Jennifer Dydyk
Editor/Editora: Tracy Nelson Maurer
Proofreader/Correctora de pruebas: Melissa Boyce
Coordinador de producción/Production manager: Candice Campbell
Translated by/Traducción de: Santiago Ochoa
Spanish-language copyediting and proofreading/ Maquetación y corrección en español: Base Tres

Hardcover 978-1-0398-6935-6
Paperback 978-1-0398-6914-1
Ebook (pdf) 978-1-0398-6956-1
Epub 978-1-0398-6977-6

Printed in the U.S.A./Impreso en los Estados Unidos/CP112025

Published in Canada
Publicado en Canadá
Crabtree Publishing
616 Welland Avenue
St. Catharines, Ontario
L2M 5V6

Published in the United States
Publicado en los Estados Unidos
Crabtree Publishing
347 Fifth Avenue
Suite 1402-145
New York, NY 10016

Library and Archives Canada Cataloguing in Publication
Available at the Library and Archives Canada

Library of Congress Cataloging-in-Publication Data
Available at the Library of Congress

Photographs/Fotografías: Cover career logo icon © Trueffelpix, diamond pattern used on cover and throughout book © Aleksandr Andrushkiv, cover photo © kievstock, tools in background and on title page © Happy_Nati, Page 4 top photo © Monkey Business Images, bottom photo © Gorodenkoff, Page 5 © Studio Romantic, Page 6 © visivastudio, Page 7 top photo © FERNANDO MACIAS ROMO, bottom photo © Marina Demeshko, Page 8 © Prostock-studio, Page 9 top photo © vhpicstock, bottom photo © Didecs, Page 10 top photo © Joshua Resnick, bottom photo © Jacob Lund, Page 11 © aster1305, Page 12 top photo © Dragan Grkic, bottom photo © Rido, Page 13 top photo © Sebastian_Photography, bottom photo © Artem Oleshko, Page 14 top photo © SofikoS, bottom photo © kievstock, Page 15 top photo © Hrecheniuk Oleksii, bottom photo © wavebreakmedia, Page 16 © Atstock Productions, YouTube and instagram logos © rvlsoft, Page 17 © photographee.eu, Page 18 top photo © YAKOBCHUK VIACHESLAV, bottom photo (across pages 18 and 19) © elRoce, Page 19 top photo © Alena Veasey, Page 20 top photo © zimmytws, bottom photo © SergeyKlopotov, Page 21 © Pixel-Shot, Page 22 top photo © Evgeny Atamanenko, bottom photo © Julia Kuzenkova, Page 23 top photo © Jacob Lund, bottom photo © Parilov, Page 24 © Tinatin, Page 25 © Iakov Filimonov, Page 26 © ronstik, Page 27 © ViDI Studio, Page 28 top photo © Hryshchyshen Serhii, bottom photo © yurakrasil, Page 29 top photo © Vagengeim, bottom photo © Pixel-Shot. All images from Shutterstock.com